Intelligent Investor:

The Ultimate Guide to Successful Investing

By

Dale Blake

Table of Contents

Introduction 5

Chapter 1. Comparison of Different Options 7

Chapter 2. Evaluating and Picking a Company For Investment 10

Chapter 3. Risk Management Tips 17

Chapter 4. Building a Successful Investing Portfolio 21

Chapter 5. Aggressive and Defensive Strategies 24

Chapter 6. Market Fluctuations 26

Conclusion 28

Thank You Page 30

Intelligent Investor: The Ultimate Guide to Successful Investing

By Dale Blake

© Copyright 2015 Dale Blake

Reproduction or translation of any part of this work beyond that permitted by section 107 or 108 of the 1976 United States Copyright Act without permission of the copyright owner is unlawful. Requests for permission or further information should be addressed to the author.

This publication is designed to provide accurate and authoritative information in regard to the subject matter covered. This work is sold with the understanding that the publisher is not engaged in rendering legal, accounting, or other professional services. If legal advice or other expert assistance is required, the services of a competent professional person should be sought.

First Published, 2015

Printed in the United States of America

Introduction

An average person spends almost more than half of his life earnings, while there are some decisions which should be taken regarding the wellbeing of your hard work of many years and this can be done through investing. It is secure way of ensuring that all the money you earned is safe and can be retrieved when in need. The value of money now is worth more than the money in future so it should be spend wisely now to have a secure future. People tend to get stressed or worry a lot when the decision of investing comes as they lack the technical knowledge so they think the decision is very difficult and risky. This is not entirely true, all you need is some basic information and a good plan to which you can stick for a time and you can take a good decision just like any professional in finance.

These things can be learned easily and their implementation is not hard either. There are bad investments too but it can be avoided by getting the right kind of fact about the market and then taking the decision based on it. The benefits of taking right decision are long lasting, you get the financial security in the unstable market and advantages can be enjoyed over a long period of time. People who has plan to invest their savings somewhere can have change of heart regarding the objectives such as capital appreciation, gaining income etc. many would advise to go for diversification as the more widespread the income the better the returns with less risk. This book intends to enlighten you with the basic knowledge about the investment so that a good decision can be made.

Chapter 1. Comparison of Different Options

The expected return associated with different options vary. There are many ways in which you can invest.

1. Single Asset Investment

In this type of investment the investor invests in one type of assets. They belong from the same category. The returns can be positive if spend in a well searched set of assets. The market is dynamic, if one thing has value today then it does not mean that it will be of such value in future because the demand can change. So the analysis should be done before choosing the type of asset. The major risk which is associated with it is that when you associate or spend all your money in one kind of assets. If their value decreases then the investor suffers a lot. When choosing the single asset things that should be considered are that trustees can overcome the problem of no diversification, the aspect of expected return are promising and the objectives associated with the investments will be fulfilled.

2. Multi Asset Portfolio Investment

This kind of investment is preferred by many because the risk associated with them is less as compared to the single asset so is the expected return. The reason is that money is invested in various kind of assets so if the value or worth of one asset decreases then the investor still can get return from other assets in which he had invested. So the diversified portfolio let him earn from others and the chances are there that of one of the asset the worth will increase in the future. Many financial people refer this kind of investment to people who do not want to put all their eggs in one basket.

The best way to do comparison is to look at the reports of the market regarding the assets or portfolios in which you want to invest. They are the good way of analyzing and evaluating how the things have worked in the past. They work as guideline as you take decision based on the past because the trends do follow similarly in the future. The data also tells which of them were risky because their trend lines have a lot of fluctuations and it becomes hard to predict what will be the return in the future. Such kind of assets should be avoided. The safe assets in which you can invest are gold, real estate and collectibles because their value increase with passage of time and one does not face any heavy losses related to them. When making the decision do consider the amount you are investing, if the amount is less then you can invest in the risky assets as the amount spend is less and the variation in expected return would not effect in a negative way. Precautions are advised to be taken when a large sum of money is being spend. Choose the assets accordingly and try to invest in the safe assets mentioned above because the expected return with them is always high due to their worth in the society and market.

Chapter 2. Evaluating and Picking a Company For Investment

The most tricky and risky decision is when you want to invest in a company. All that glitters is not gold can be applied here because you may think a company has a good brand name in the market and many know about then it must be a good option for investing. The reality might be quite different than what you perceive because a company will never reveal to investors the problems they are facing and at what point in the market they are financially standing. It has been seen in the past that the companies people thought were going very well were suddenly bankrupt. This does not happen overnight. The problems prevail till such an extent that the company has to shut down and the investor and general public come to know about it very late. So from the start evaluate the company properly and pick the company wisely. Below, the description is given which tells how to pick and evaluate a company.

With the emergence of internet the information has become very common and it accessible by many all over the globe. All kind of people can evaluate them regardless of their profession or from where they belong. Due to the travelling of information in quickly around the world the stock has become volatile as compared to the past and their evaluation has changed too. However, the criteria of evaluating a company has not changed. It is based on the ROE (return on equity), earning and the value of company with comparison with other companies.

Earnings is an important criteria to judge the performance of a company. It indicates the running of it and how much it is getting in return with respect to what it is investing. Stocks should be bought in the companies which has the chance of future earnings. Earnings, further can be divided into three sub categories through which the growth can be judged. The three subcategories are stability, quality and growth.

The earnings growth is mostly presented in percentages based on the data by per annum, quarterly and month wise. The assumption associated with it is the growth should increase with respect to the previous time period by which the comparison is being done. The critics say that this is all about past and it is not necessary that similar patterns would prevail in the future as well. According to them the focus should be on the future. This statement is true to some extent but the past records have their own significance because they represent how the company was doing. If a company has good history then it will have a good future. Things can change in the future but it would be risky to invest while knowing the past record was not good. The history depicts the ability of the company to grow in the future.

The growth pattern is important and it should be compared with the market as well. For example if a company has a growth rate of 4% while the market is growing at the rate of 8% then the company is lacking behind and it would not be a wise decision to invest in it. On the other hand if the company is growing at 8% while the market has a growth rate of 4% then it would be wise to invest in the company. Thus, such comparisons are important while looking at the earnings growth.

The consistency of the company with regard to their growth can be judged by the earnings stability. It tells whether the company was able to sustain its growth over the passage of time. These type of earnings are maintained by companies who have a predictable pattern of growth. The stability can come from top line or bottom line depending the way the company is operating. So do verify from where there is growth in the company before taking the decision to invest.

Last subcategory of the earning is the earnings quality which tells the status of the company. This is mostly done by professionals so their services should be acquired when taking the decision. If such facility is not available then you can do analysis yourself based on some steps. For example if a company's earning is growing but the revenues are declining and costs are increasing, this shows there is deviation from the accounting standard and such growth will not last long. So it should be avoided.

ROE (return on equity) calculates the effectiveness of the managers in turning the profits based on the money the shareholders of the company has invested. ROE helps in the relative valuation. It can also be used to do the comparison with the market as a whole and also with the relatable groups, industries and sectors. If there would not be any earning then it would be negative. As with the case of earnings growth same case is with the ROE i.e. the historical trend should be seen and analyzed and then the decision should be taken. If the historical data shows the increasing trend then investments should be made. Do look for the relative comparison with the other companies dealing in the market and then decision should be taken.

There are other factors and steps that should be taken when evaluating and then picking the company because you cannot rely on just few facts, terms or personal likeness of the company. Investing in the stocks can be tricky. A good investigation includes looking at the history, trends and financial reports. The financial reports includes balance sheet, income and expense statements, cash flows statements and shareholders' equity report. Companies do produce their financial reports annually so they can be easily accessible and judged. Following are the main factors that should be considered when thinking about investing.

You should see if the company has potential in increasing the revenues in the future, at the same time the costs should be kept low. Companies that are indulged in innovation are predicted to have a high growth rate in the future as their sales increase when they make products according to the demand of the customers so their worth increases in the market. There should be safe exit and if you want to exit from the company then the value you invested must be returned equally or more according to the valuation in the investment. Also look for companies that do not require large sum of investments initially so that you do not risk the large sum and learn with small investments first.

One factor which is mostly overlooked by many are the management of the company. This factor is very important because only an excellent management with knowledge, experience and skills help a company to grow. If the people at the base and bottom are not good then the company cannot progress over time. The plan, mission and objective should be realistic of the company that can be achieved in the future.

The annual reports also give the hints what the company is facing in the current marketplaces and at which place it stands. It also tell what future actions and plans are made to increase the profits and revenues in the future. One important thing to notice is that whether the company is investing in the only in one asset or have they spread the investments over different sources. Also, the economy should be considered regarding the industry in which the company is operating. Do look if the company is operating in which the economy is strong or the one in which it is deteriorating. Some companies have the potential to cope the varying situations and they come out of it without effecting the company.

Leadership of the company also matters a lot. A company with strong and motivated leadership can lead the company towards growth and success. They increase the shareholders' value and the worth of their stock price. They maintain a strong position in the market. The stock price should be seen over past few years. If they had been increasing then it is good but if they had been fluctuating or decreasing then there will be risk involved with them.

Chapter 3. Risk Management Tips

You should be smart while investing. The risk management tips tell how to avoid the risk. There are different strategies that can be followed to avert the risk to the minimum.

1. The basic strategy to avoid risk is to make the portfolio as diverse as possible so that if the prices of one asset such as gold decreases then you would not face major losses as your portfolio also has many other assets in your portfolio. Invest in the various type of sectors so that the assets would not be interlinked or related. For example invest in technology, industrial goods, services and healthcare. This would insure the less volatility of the stocks due to less connectivity the stocks. When an industry gets effected it also takes down the companies operating in those companies so the best strategy to follow is to invest in different industries rather than the companies.

2. A company can face many surprises that is the unexpected situations which can directly affect your investment. So whenever choosing the company look for the limited coverage, inconsistent analysis and new company. A company having limited coverage will have more risk due to less widespread, with less proper analysis will result in fabricated data which would not let you to take proper decision and a new company is at risk itself i.e. whether they will succeed in the future or not.

3. Do the analysis of the earnings. To do this get the historical data via the annual reports and only invest it there is an increasing rate and less fluctuations.

4. Beta analysis is another way of analyzing the risk. The company is volatile if the beta is high. It basically says that the stocks are related to the market generally. A low beta will earn less in bull cycle but it would not lose with significant amount in bear cycle. Choose the beta with low rate which operates in the bigger market. It is based on the performance in the past only so this strategy can be used with some other strategy.

5. Price to earnings ratio can be used in deciding. Generally an investor thinks that if the profit is more than the price of the share then it is not a good deal and there might be some problem associated with it.

When the P/E ratio is low, it indicates that the company can be in trouble. If the stocks seem to be cheap due to P/E ratio then there would not be good rate of return. So such kind of companies have risk associated with them.

6. There are companies known as "Glamor Companies" which have a high growth rate of stocks with volatility. Many people forecast that in the future there would be increasing growth but it is not true in all cases. All they see is a new company with impressive goals, strategy and objectives which they think would be successful but things can turn bad resulting in the loss. There is too much optimism linked to them which can be unrealistic. The problems with these companies are the financial problems, limited forces which limits their growth, inadequate staff and skills, lack of experience of the management and less liquidity of buying new assets and payroll. So precaution should be taken while thinking about such companies. There are wide spread of these companies and market failure is also high in these kind of companies. So it is advisable to not invest in them if you do not know the proper information regarding them.

All the above mentioned strategies regarding the minimizing of the risk should be considered and followed to reduce the risk as much as possible.

Chapter 4. Building a Successful Investing Portfolio

There are five main steps that can be taken to make the portfolio successful.

1. Set the Financial Objectives

You have to decide from the two choices that which one you want to choose based on the type of investment you intend to do. The two choices are either capital growth or income from the investment. Those who chose the income should think about the equity income funds, the investment is done with the company who can pay the dividends to their shareholders. Strategic bond funds allow the investor to invest in the high yielding bonds which reduces the risk with the increase in the interest rate.

2. Your approach towards the risk

It is the law that with high returns high risk is associated and with low return low risk is associated. Now the decision is with you, if you want more returns then invest in the different companies of the industries which have high risk and vice versa. The type of portfolio is based on how much you can invest in the different assets. When making the portfolio do keep in mind the amount of volatility you can afford. Risk is also related to the time period of the investment. For shorter period of time consider the less volatile portfolio and if you want to invest for longer time then volatile portfolio can be made.

3. Select the asset allocation

For a balanced portfolio consists of widely spreading the portfolio into equities, bonds, stocks, property, return funds and cash. These different kind of investments will have different effect on the return of the investment so the portfolio should be divided in a way that it consists of such various options and not just one or two. It helps to reduce risk, volatility and losses. It even gives more opportunities to the investor.

4. Selection of the Fund

When the assets allocation is finalized by the investor he should decide which funds to include in the portfolio. You can make a managed portfolio or pick the funds belonging to diverse asset class.

5. Review of the Portfolio

Before actually investing, based on the portfolio you have made, recheck it properly. Eliminate anything which you think will cause loss or is more risky. With time to time the portfolio should be assessed so that the progress can be checked. If they see that some of the funds are not doing good then it can be excluded or new ones can be bought to make the portfolio more successful.

Chapter 5. Aggressive and Defensive Strategies

Aggressive Investing Strategy

It is a kind of portfolio management strategy that is used to increase the profits by taking high risks. Its primary objective is about capital appreciation not the safety or income. People who are ready to take the risk for more returns choose this strategy. It is based on the high risk asset and high reward for e.g. commodities and equities in the portfolio. It generally consist of the stocks.

The advantages of this strategy is that the returns are high. If you invest in them then you can get profit and the value of your portfolio will be more. The main disadvantage associated with it is that there is a lot of risk associated with it which can either give you profit or losses.

Defensive Investing Strategy

It is considered to be the conservative strategy in which one is totally risk averse. You only invest in those areas where there is guarantee of getting the promised return. The portfolio is rebalanced at regular basis to ward off the risk. The investment is done in short maturity bonds and blue chip stocks. The portfolio is kept diverse so that they do not invest in one area only because that is risky. This strategy is adopted to avoid the losses.

The advantage of this strategy is that it helps to prevent the unnecessarily risk. The losses are less due to the diversified portfolio. The returns are generally moderate. The disadvantage is that many opportunities are not availed because they were considered risky but in reality they could have proven to be more profitable. The chance of earning more is also not taken wisely.

Chapter 6. Market Fluctuations

The market is very dynamic, it never remains static. The market works on the base of supply and demand by the consumers. If the demand of something decreases then the companies operating in them suffers as they lose their customers and if the demand increases then there is boom in the industry because companies start to earn more. The supply is adjusted according to the demand. The fluctuations can be seen by taking note that how the need, taste and demand of consumer is in the recent time. Companies in the market are working towards providing the solutions to the problems of the customers because these help them to increase their sales, market share and make their company strong. According to Warren Buffet the market fluctuation should be seen as friends. The reason is that they can create opportunity for you if see it wisely and closely.

One should try to invest more in the companies whose demand is more in the market and it would be in the future as well. If you have invested in the some company and due to fluctuations in the market you can reap the profits if fluctuation had caused any positive results. However if you were planning to invest and then due to the market fluctuation the price increased then you would face loss as you would have to pay more now.

The fluctuations can be analyzed based on the market. As mentioned above the fluctuations are relative. It effects people in very different ways. It depends whether the person who got effected is a buyer or seller as the dynamics are somewhat dissimilar. Data can be taken from the market reports of the stock exchange. All the information is available on the internet so no extra efforts are required to make to get the reports. The track of the market should be noted on daily basis so that you can know how things are being turned out.

Conclusion

The investment word itself suggests that some risk is associated with it. There is no such thing as riskless investment because market is dynamic with changes coming overnight. Everything has become so much fast paced that there is no guarantee of static situations, they are supposed to change. In this kind of environment the decision of investment should be taken wisely. There are many options available such as investing in stocks, bonds, equities shares etc.

Many different suggestions are given in the book related to the creation of portfolio and the assets that should be included. You should choose the strategy depending upon the amount that can be spent in the investment and how much risk that you can take with regard to that. The portfolio should be balanced and successful so that you earn the profits on it. The most important part of investment is choosing the right company when investing in their shares or stock. Go for the one with a strong financial background. Consult the authentic and professional people for the advice.

In the end the decision is yours, so do all the research you can before taking any decision.

Thank You Page

I want to personally thank you for reading my book. I hope you found information in this book useful and I would be very grateful if you could leave your honest review about this book. I certainly want to thank you in advance for doing this.

If you have the time, you can check my other books too.

www.ingramcontent.com/pod-product-compliance
Lightning Source LLC
LaVergne TN
LVHW021747060526
838200LV00052B/3516